The Story of a Special Day
Volume 52

February
21

The 52ⁿᵈ day of the year. There are 313 days (314 in leap years) remaining until the end of the year.

by Michael Dobson

Timespinner
Press

This book is also available in e-book form for Kindle, e-pub devices, and other formats from your favorite online booksellers.

For more information about the series, about us, or about your special day, please email us at editor@timespinnerpress.com.

Look for other volumes in *The Story of a Special Day*, coming often. See www.timespinnerpress.com for details and for the most recent information.

Table of Contents

For the definition of "O.S.," "N.S.," "CE," and "BCE" used with some dates , see the section "On Names and Dates."

Cover: The Washington Monument and Reflecting Pool, by Carol M. Highsmith. The Washington Monument was dedicated on February 21, 1885 — the **Event of the Day**.

Quote of the Day

"An essential aspect of creativity is not being afraid to fail."

Edwin H. Land, inventor of the first practical instant camera and co-founder of the Polaroid Corporation. The Polaroid Land Camera was demonstrated publicly for the first time on February 21, 1947

Today
in
History

CHEM
ACU
MAGNA

February 21

The Washington Monument (Courtesy National Park Service)

Event of the Day
February 21, 1885 — Washington Monument Dedicated

In his eulogy, General "Light-Horse Harry" Lee described George Washington in the famous words, "First in war, first in peace, and first in the hearts of his countrymen."

The dominant military and political leader of the newly-independent United States of America, George Washington was described as the "greatest character of the age" by none other than King George III, his enemy in the Revolutionary War. A number of monuments and statues to George Washington can be found around the country, but by far the most famous is the Washington Monument in the nation's capital.

The Controversy

The new nation's Congress approved a monument in Washington's honor, but in 1801, they cancelled it.

Although Washington himself opposed the idea of political parties, he had in fact become the symbol of the Federalist Party, which advocated a strong national government to promote economic growth. On the other side was Thomas Jefferson's Democratic-Republican Party, which opposed centralization and also contained many who had opposed the new Constitution in the first place.

In 1801, the Democratic-Republicans swept both houses of Congress and their leader Thomas Jefferson became President. They no longer wished to honor someone identified with the other party. In addition, Jefferson, among others, thought that the idea of monuments to powerful men was not in line with Republican values. His party not only cancelled the proposed monument, but also blocked the use of Washington's image on coins and the celebration of his birthday.

Robert Mills' winning design for the Washington Monument. Note the different shape of the obelisk and the addition of the large colonnade at the bottom.

Design and Fundraising

It was not until 1832, the 100th anniversary of Washington's birth, that the Washington National Monument Society was born. By 1836, the group raised $28,000 — the equivalent to $17 million in 2015. They created a design competition for the new monument, according to the following criteria.

> It is proposed that the contemplated monument shall be like him in whose honor it is to be constructed, unparalleled in the world, and commensurate with the gratitude, liberality, and patriotism of the people by whom it is to be erected ... [It] should blend stupendousness with elegance, and be of such magnitude and beauty as to be an object of pride to the American people, and of admiration to all who see it. Its material is intended to be wholly American, and to be of marble and granite brought from each state, that each state may participate in the glory of contributing material as well as in funds to its construction.

Architect Robert Mills had an advantage: he had already designed a Washington Monument for the city of Baltimore, Maryland, which was completed in 1829. This was the first major monument built to honor the first President.

The design for the proposed monument (left) was a tall obelisk surrounded by a colonnade that would contain statues of 30 Revolutionary War heroes.

The estimated price tag of $1 million (over $600 million in 2015) was far more than the Society had anticipated, but they decided to move forward with the obelisk portion — hoping that further donations would make it possible to complete the project.

The original site for the Washington Monument was meant to be where a line running south from the White House would cross a line running west from the Capitol, but the ground was too unstable to support the massive monument. As a result, the site was moved 390 feet. A small monolith marks the original location on the National Mall.

Construction Begins

By now, the Society had raised some $86,000, enough to begin construction in 1848, but by 1854 the money was all spent and the monument was only 152 feet high. A stone for the new monument that had been donated by Pope Pius IX was destroyed by members of the American Party, an anti-Catholic and nativist political party commonly known as the "Know-Nothings." The resultant clash caused donations to dry up altogether.

The Society appealed to Congress for funding, but the Know-Nothings took control of the group, causing Congress to immediately drop the issue. The new leadership tried to continue construction, but only managed to add four feet to the height of the memorial. Meanwhile, the original Society fought back against the takeover, and control of the Monument shifted back and forth until the general disintegration of the Know-Nothings also dissolved their Monument Society.

The beginnings of the American Civil War in 1861 stopped further work altogether.

The partially completed Washington Monument circa 1860 (Photo: Mathew Brady/Levin Handy)

Completion and Dedication

After the end of the Civil War, interest in the Washington Monument resurfaced. In 1876, the Centennial of the Declaration of Independence, Congress appropriated another $200,000 to resume construction. The project almost immediately bogged down again in a discussion about design. More and more people thought a simple obelisk, without the colonnade, would be appropriate, although Robert Mills, unsurprisingly, objected, saying that omitting the colonnade would make the monument look like a stalk of asparagus.

Five new designs were considered, and finally the Society decided to abandon the colonnade and alter the shape of the obelisk so it would have classical Egyptian proportions. In 1879, construction restarted. Army Corps of Engineers Colonel Thomas Casey redesigned the foundation so it would support the more than 40,000 ton weight of the structure. Because he needed to acquire marble from other quarries, the bottom third of the monument is slightly lighter in shade than the rest.

The remainder of the construction took only four years, with the cast aluminum lightning rod added on December 6, 1884. At the time, aluminum was a precious metal, with a price comparable to silver. The 100-ounce lightning rod was at the time the largest single piece of aluminum ever cast.

On February 21, 1885, the new Washington Monument was dedicated. President Chester A. Arthur said, "I do now...in behalf of the people, receive this monument...and declare it dedicated from this time forth to the immortal name and memory of George Washington."

The Monument

At the time of its completion, the Washington Monument was, at 554 feet, the new record holder for tallest building in the world, which had previously been held by the Cologne (Germany) Cathedral. It lost the title in 1889 with the completion of the Eiffel Tower.

Putting the aluminum capstone on the Washington Monument, from
Harper's Weekly, 1884

Over 10,000 people climbed the 898 steps to the
top in the first six months after its dedication. When
the freight elevator used in construction was
reconfigured for passengers, attendance skyrocketed,
with 55,000 visitors each month by 1888. By 1979,
attendance exceeded 1 million visitors per year.

In 1982, a man named Norman Mayer held the Monument hostage, claiming that the van he was driving was filled with explosives, a claim later found to be false.

From 1998 to 2001, it was closed and covered in scaffolding for an extensive restoration. Following the September 11 terrorist attacks, the monument was closed again until it could be renovated to provide increased security. In 2001, a 5.8 magnitude earthquake caused numerous cracks in the monument, causing another period of closing while repairs were made.

Today, the Washington Monument is one of the iconic symbols of the US capital city, instantly recognizable worldwide.

A diagram of the world's tallest buildings in 1884 by George Cram. Note the Washington Monument in the center background.

A young girl looks at the Washington Monument and the Reflecting Pool on the National Mall in Washington, DC. (Photo: Nebiyu Samuel, CC BY-SA 4.0)

A replica of the "Puffing Devil" created by the Trevithick Society, Cornwall, United Kingdom (Photo: Chris Allen, CC BY-SA 2.0)

What Happened on February 21?

From great works of engineering and art, to devastating wars and natural disasters, thousands of years of history have left their mark on each and every day of the year. Here are some important events that occurred on February 21. (Items with a photo or illustration are boxed.)

1804 — The **first** full-scale working railway **steam locomotive**, the "Puffing Devil," built by Richard Trevithick, makes its maiden run from the Pen-y-darren ironworks to Abercynon in South Wales.

1828 — The **first Native American newspaper**, the *Cherokee Phoenix* (ᏣᎳᎩ ᏓᎳᏗᎤᎯᏌᏅᎯ, *Tsalagi Tsulehisanvhi*) publishes its first issue. It is also the first newspaper published in a Native American language. The newspaper ceased publication in 1834, but was revived in the 20th century in both print and on-line versions.

1848 — German political philosophers Karl Marx and Friedrich Engels publish *The Communist Manifesto.*

1880 — The **first telephone directory**, consisting of 50 individuals and businesses in New Haven, Connecticut, is published.

1916 — World War I's **Battle of Verdun** begins. The longest and one of the most costly battles in history, lasting 303 days and costing more than 300,000 lives.

1918 — The **last Carolina parakeet** (*Conuropsis carolinensis*), the only indigenous parrot native to the eastern and central United States, dies in captivity at the Cincinnati Zoo.

Carolina Parakeet (Photo: James St. John, CC BY-SA 2.0)

1925 — The **first issue of** *The New Yorker* magazine, which becomes one of the most influential magazines in the US, is published.

1947 — The **first instant (Polaroid) camera,** designed by inventor Edwin Land, is demonstrated publicly for the first time at a meeting of the Optical Society of America.

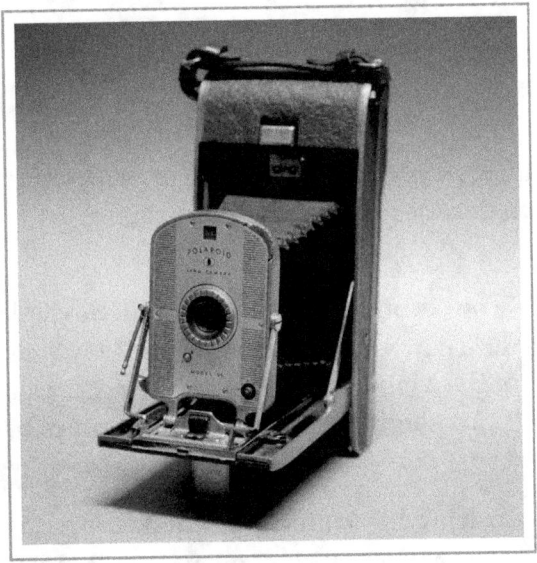

First commercially available Polaroid Land Camera

1948 — **NASCAR,** the National Association for Stock Car Auto Racing, is founded. Today it is second only to the National Football League in US sports popularity.

1958 — Graphic designer Gerald Holtom designs the **peace symbol** for the Campaign for Nuclear Disarmament (CND). The symbol is based on the semaphore signals for the letters "N" and "D"

1972 — US President Richard M. **Nixon visits** the People's Republic of **China**, a critical step in the normalization of Sino-America relations after more than two decades of non-communication.

1972 — The second of three successful Soviet lunar sample return missions, **Luna 20**, lands on the surface of the Moon. The next day, its ascent stage blasts off carrying 30 grams of lunar samples back to Earth.

1975 — During the **Watergate scandal**, former Attorney General John Mitchell and White House aides H. R. Haldeman and John Erlichman are sentenced to prison.

1995 — Steve Fossett becomes the **first person to fly solo across the Pacific Ocean in a balloon.**

Mao Zedong and Richard Nixon in China, 1972

Quote of the Day

"Among those whom I like or admire, I can find no common denominator, but among those whom I love, I can: all of them make me laugh."

W. H. Auden, poet
born February 21, 1907

Births
and
Deaths

February 21

Malcolm X, civil rights activist, assassinated February 21, 1965. (Photo: Herman Hiller, NYWTS)

Notable February 21 People

With the current world population at about seven billion people, on average about 19 million people also celebrate their birthdays on February 21 — and that isn't counting millions and millions who came before! No matter when you were born, you share your birthday with many special people whose accomplishments (and occasionally embarrassments) have been noted as part of history.

In this section, you'll meet fascinating people who share your birthday. They're organized by what they're famous for, and then in reverse chronological order from most recent to earliest. Those who are shown in photographs or artwork have a box around them. We don't have photos of everyone, so please forgive us if your favorite person is missing.

Some of these people you've heard of, others will be new to you, but they all make up an important part of the reason that February 21 is a truly special day!

Official Congressional portraits of John Lewis and Barbara Jordan

Who Was Born on February 21?

Business and Fashion

David Geffen, entertainment magnate who founded or co-founded such companies as Asylum Records, Geffen Records, and DreamWorks. *(1943)*

Hubert de Givenchy, fashion designer who founded the House of Givenchy; designed the wardrobes of such notables as First Lady Jacqueline Kennedy and actress Audrey Hepburn. *(1927)*

Charles Scribner I, co-founded the publishing company later known as Charles Scribner's Sons. *(1821)*

Government and Military

John Lewis, politician and civil rights activist, member of Congress from Georgia, and winner of the Presidential Medal of Freedom. *(1940)*

Harald V, King of Norway and Olympic competitor in sailing. *(1937)*

Barbara Jordan, politician and civil rights activist; first southern African-American woman elected to the US Congress; winner of the Presidential Medal of Freedom. *(1936)*

Robert Mugabe, revolutionary and controversial head of state of Zimbabwe since 1980. *(1924)*

Ilmari Juutilainen, Finnish fighter pilot who became the top scoring non-German fighter ace of all time, with 94 confirmed victories. *(1914)*[*]

Korechika Anami (阿南 惟幾), Japanese army leader who served as War Minister at the time of the Japanese surrender. *(1887)*

Antonio López de Santa Anna, Mexican politician and general known as the "Napoleon of the West; served eleven non-consecutive terms as president of his country. Although his forces were victorious at the Battle of the Alamo, he lost his fight to prevent the establishment of the Republic of Texas. *(1794)*

Antonio López de Santa Anna

---

[*] Juutilainen died in 1999 on the same date he was born.

Journalism and Literature

David Foster Wallace, novelist best known for *Infinite Jest* and *The Pale King. (1962)*

Chuck Palahniuk, novelist and journalist best known for writing the novel *Fight Club,* which subsequently became a film. *(1962)*

Richard A. Lupoff, science fiction and mystery writer. *(1935)*

Erma Bombeck, humorist known for her long-running humor column about suburban home life. *(1927)*

W. H. Auden, English-American poet sometimes called "the 20th century's greatest poet." *(1904)*

W. H. Auden
(Photo: Carl Van Vechten)

Anaïs Nin, essayist known for her extensive diaries and journals, as well as for her erotic writings. *(1903)*

Music

Mary Chapin Carpenter, country musician who won five Grammys; member of the Nashville Songwriters Hall of Fame. *(1958)*

Vince Welnick, keyboardist known for his work with the Tubes and the Grateful Dead. *(1951)*

Jerry Harrison, played keyboards and guitar for the band Talking Heads. *(1949)*

Nina Simone, singer-songwriter known for her rendition of "I Loves You, Porgy;" member of the Grammy Hall of Fame. *(1933)*

Andrés Segovia, Spanish classical guitarist regarded as one of the greatest of all time. *(1893)*

Performing Arts

Sophie Turner, actress who played Sansa Stark in the television series *Game of Thrones.* *(1996)*

Ellen Page, actress known for her Oscar nominated role in 2007's *Juno,* and as Kitty Pryde in the *X-Men* film series. *(1987)*

Jordan Peele, actor and comedian known for the TV series *Key & Peele* and *Fargo.* *(1979)*

Jennifer Love Hewitt, actress known for her role as Sarah on the TV series *Party of Five* and the horror film *I Know What You Did Last Summer.* (1979)

Aunjanue Ellis, actress known for roles in *Men of Honor, The Help,* and the TV series *High Incident.* (1969)

William Baldwin, actor known for *Flatliners,* and for television series including *Dirty Sexy Money* and *Gossip Girl;* brother of actors Alec, Daniel, and Stephen Baldwin. (1963)

Christopher Atkins, actor best known for co-starring with Brooke Shields in the 1980 film *The Blue Lagoon.* (1961)

Kelsey Grammer, actor best known as Dr. Frasier Crane on the sitcoms *Cheers* and *Frasier;* voice of Sideshow Bob on *The Simpsons.* (1955)

William Petersen, actor best known as Gil on the TV series *CSI.* (1953)

Christine Ebersole, actress and singer known for her Tony-winning Broadway work and as a cast member of *Saturday Night Live.* (1953)

Larry Drake, actor best known for playing Benny on the television series *L.A. Law.* (1949)

Alan Rickman, actor known for playing Hans Gruber in *Die Hard,* Snape in the *Harry Potter* film series, and many other roles. (1946)

Ann Sheridan

Anthony Daniels, actor and mime best known for playing C-3PO in the *Star Wars* film series. *(1946)*

Tyne Daly, actress best known for her co-starring role in the 1980s TV series *Cagney & Lacey*. *(1946)*

Rue McClanahan, actress known for her Emmy-winning role as Blanche on *The Golden Girls*. *(1934)*

Chesperito, Mexican screenwriter, actor, and comedian whose pseudonym means "Little Shakespeare," famous for such TV series as *El Chavo del Ocho* and *El Chapulín Colorado*. *(1927)*

Sam Peckinpah, director and screenwriter best known for such films as *The Wild Bunch, Straw Dogs,* and *Pat Garrett and Billy the Kid*. *(1925)*

Lucille Bremer, actress known for *Meet Me in St. Louis* and *Yolanda and the Thief*. *(1917)*

Ann Sheridan, American actress known for roles in such films as *Angels With Dirty Faces, Kings Row,* and *I Was a Male War Bride*. *(1915)*

Record Setters

Mark and Scott Kelly, American astronauts who are the only known siblings to have both traveled in space. Mark Kelly's spouse Gabrielle Giffords was a member of Congress shot in an assassination attempt in 2011. *(1964)*

Jeanne Louis Calment, French supercentenarian with the longest confirmed human lifespan on record, 122 years and 164 days. *(1875)*

Science and Technology

Henrik Dam, Danish biochemist who shared the 1943 Nobel Prize in Medicine for the discovery of Vitamin K and its role in human physiology. *(1895)*

Sir Francis Ronalds, creator of the first working electric telegraph. *(1788)*

Sports

Franklin Gutiérrez, center and right fielder for the Cleveland Indians and Seattle Mariners. *(1983)*

Braylon Edwards, wide receiver for the Cleveland Browns, New York Jets, and other teams. *(1983)*

Ryan Smyth, ice hockey player best known for his years with the Edmonton Oilers; captain of Canada's world championship hockey team for a record-setting six years. *(1976)*

Leroy Burrell, American track and field athlete who won a gold medal in the 1992 Olympic Games. *(1967)*

Alan Trammell, shortstop, manager, and coach with the Detroit Tigers. *(1958)*

Bob Ryan, sportswriter who received the 2015 PEN/ESPN Lifetime Achievement Award for Literary Sports Writing. *(1946)*

Jack Ramsay, basketball coach for the Portland Trail Blazers and other teams, named to the Naismith Memorial Basketball Hall of Fame. *(1925)*

Ryan Smyth (Photo: Lisa Gansky, CC BY-SA 3.0)

Baruch Spinoza, philosopher. Spinoza died February 21, 1677

Who Died on February 21?

Activism

Malcolm X, American civil rights activist, assassinated after disavowing the African-American Nation of Islam, of which he had previously been a leader. *(1965)* *(Photo page 18.)*

Augusto Sandino, Nicaraguan revolutionary leader opposing the US military occupation of that country; named a national hero by the Nicaraguan congress. *(1934)*

Business

Barney Rosset, owned Grove Press; won legal battles to publish unexpurgated versions of *Lady Chatterley's Lover* and *Tropic of Cancer* in an important Supreme Court ruling for free speech. *(2012)*

Tim Horton, Canadian ice hockey player who co-founded the restaurant chain of the same name. *(1974)*

Crime and Punishment

Robert O. Marshall, convicted of the contract killing of his wife, subject of the book and miniseries *Blind Faith*. *(2015)*

Literature

Mikhail Sholokov (Михаи́л Шо́лохов), Soviet-era Russian novelist who won the 1965 Nobel Prize in Literature; best known for the book *And Quiet Flows the Don*. *(1984)*

Military

Eric Brown, most decorated pilot in the history of the British Royal Navy; set world records for (among others) the most different types of aircraft flown (487) and most aircraft carrier deck takeoffs and landings (2,407 and 2,271). *(2016)*

Ilmari Juutilainen, Finnish fighter pilot who became the top scoring non-German fighter ace of all time, with 94 confirmed victories. *(1999)*[†]

Music

Morton Gould, composer and conducter who won the 1995 Pulitzer Prize in Music for Stringmusic; received the 2005 Grammy Lifetime Achievement Award. *(1996)*

[†] Juutilainen was born in 1914 on the same date that he died.

Performing Arts

Ben Chapman, played the Gill-Man in the 1954 horror film *Creature from the Black Lagoon. (2008)*

Gill-Man (played by **Ben Chapman**) menaces Julie Adams in the 1954 film *Creature from the Black Lagoon.*

Philosophy

Baruch Spinoza, philosopher considered one of the most important of the 17th century. *(1677)* *(Photo page 30.)*

Science

Gertrude B. Elion, biochemist who shared the 1988 Nobel Prize in Medicine for developing important new drugs. *(1999)*

Inge Lehmann, Danish seismologist who made the discovery that the Earth had a solid inner core inside a molten outer core; at 104 years of age, she was the longest-lived woman scientist in history. *(1993)*

Howard Florey, Australian researcher who shared the 1945 Nobel Prize in Medicine for his role in the development of penicillin. *(1968)*

Sir Frederick Banting, Canadian medical scientist who shared the 1923 Nobel Prize in Medicine for the discovery of insulin; youngest Nobel laureate ever in his category. *(1941)*

George Hale, astronomer known for overseeing the planning and construction of some of the largest optical telescopes in the world, including the 200-inch Hale reflecting telescope at Palomar Observatory. *(1938)*

Heike Kamerlingh Omnes, received the 1913 Nobel Prize in Physics for his work with extreme low temperatures, which resulted in the first liquification of helium and the discovery of superconductivity. *(1926)*

Sports

Eric Liddell, Scottish athlete who won a gold medal at the 1924 Olympics; portrayed in the 1981 Oscar-winning film *Chariots of Fire.* *(1945)*

Eric Liddell

Ferenc Szisz, Hungarian race car driver who won the first Grand Prix race in 1906. *(1944)*

Quote of the Day

"You cannot save people, you can only love them."

Anaïs Nin, writer, born February 21, 1903

Holidays
Around
the World

February 21

Michael Dobson

For **National Margarita Weekend**, the third weekend in February.
(Photo: "Cocktail Marler," CC BY-SA 3.0)

Holidays Around the World

If you're looking for a reason to take your special day off, you should know that every single day is a holiday somewhere in the world! Here's some of what you can celebrate on February 21!

General Events

International Mother Language Day (United Nations)/Language Martyr's Day (Bangladesh)

The United Nations established this observance, held each February 21, to promote awareness of linguistic and cultural diversity, multilinguism, and the preservation of less common languages.

The date was chosen to honor the deaths of students killed by police while demonstrating to have Bengali recognized as one of the official languages of East Pakistan (today's Bangladesh).

In that country, it is observed as ভাষা আন্দোলন দিবস, or *Bhasha Andolôn Dibôs*, which means Language Movement/Martyr's Day.

Armed Forces Day (South Africa)

Many nations choose a day each year to honor their armed forces. In South Africa, the date commemorates the February 21, 1993, reconstitution of the South African Defense Force into its current identity. Parades are held nationwide.

King's Birthday (Norway)

The birthday of the reigning king or queen is usually celebrated in countries where there is a monarchy. King Harald V of Norway was born February 21, 1937. *(See page 21.)*

Food Days

In the United States, almost every day of the year is dedicated to a particular food. (Some other countries also have official food days, but only in America is there one every single day!) Sponsored by manufacturers, retailers, farmers, or simply fans, these days are often proclaimed by the President, Congress, state governors, or mayors. Given that there are more different foods than days of the year, some days honor more than one kind of food!

According to Foodimentary, February 21 is both **National Sticky Bun Day** and **National Biscuits and Gravy Day.** Be sure not to get them mixed up.

If February 21 happens to fall on the third weekend of the month, it's also **National Margarita Weekend**. If you choose to waste away looking for your lost shaker of salt, be sure to avoid driving. *(Photo page 38.)*

Food Months

The entire month of February is used to celebrate numerous foods. Here's what to eat in February!

- Canned Food Month
- Grapefruit Month
- National Chocolate Lovers Month
- National Cherry Month
- National Grapefruit Month
- National Snack Food Month
- National Potato Lovers Month
- Return Shopping Carts to the Supermarket Month
- National Hot Breakfast Month

An abandoned shopping cart, by Michiel1972 (CC BY-SA 3.0) for
Return Shopping Carts to the Supermarket Month

Religious Feast Days and Holidays

Ash Wednesday/Shrove Tuesday

The Lenten season prior to Easter has events that sometimes fall on February 21. In the Netherlands, Shrove Tuesday is celebrated as **National Pancake Day**. In Latvia, the festival of **Meteņi** ends on Ash Wednesday. Of course, Shrove Tuesday is also the occasion of **Mardi Gras.**

Mardi Gras

French for "Fat Tuesday," this celebration takes place the day before Ash Wednesday, the beginning of the Lenten season. The New Orleans Mardi Gras celebration is perhaps the most famous, but Mardi Gras and the Carnival season (between Ephiphany and Ash Wednesday) are celebrated in many areas with large Catholic populations. It's known as *Karneval* or *Fasching* in Germany, *Martedi Grasso* in Italy, and *Fettisdagen* in Sweden.

Mardi Gras can take place anywhere from February 3 to March 9 in regular years, and from February 4 to March 9 in leap years.

Lent

Ash Wednesday begins the season of Lent, a period of prayer and self-denial commemorating the 40 days Jesus spent fasting in the desert, can begin any day between February 4 and March 10 in common years, and as late as March 11 in leap years. The exact beginning of Lent is calculated differently by different Christian denominations.

Sheet music for the "Mardi Gras Rag," 1914

Saint Days

Each day in the year is considered a feast day for one or more saints. They are somewhat different in western Christianity (Catholicism and many forms of Protestantism) and in eastern (Orthodox) Christianity.

In *Western Christianity*, it is the feast day of Saints Pepin of Landen, Peter Damian, and Randoald of Grandval.

In *Eastern Orthodox Christianity*, it is also the commemoration of Saints Eustathius of Antioch, Maximianus of Ravenna, John Scholasticus, Zachariah Patriarch of Jerusalem, George of Amastris, Felix of Metz, Severus, Alexander of Adrumetum, Paterius, Ercongotha, Gundebert, Germanus of Granfelden, Avitus II of Clermont, Valerius, and Macarius. (These saints are commemorated on February 8 by "Old Calendrists‡.")

Honorary Months

Presidents, Congresses, and nations around the world issue proclamations recognizing particular months to honor certain causes. These events generally fall in February, though honorary months do come and go. Holidays established by states and nonprofit organizations are listed if verified. If not otherwise specified, all are US.

---

‡ "Old Calendrists" use the Julian calendar rather than the modern Gregorian calendar. See "What Day of the Week is February 21?"

Black History Month (United States, Canada)

One of the most famous honorary months is Black History Month (sometimes African-American History Month). During Black History Month, important people and events in the African diaspora are commemorated. In the US and Canada, Black History Month is observed in February; in the UK, it's October.

"The First Vote," by Alfred Waud (1867), for **Black History Month**

Other honorary month designations for February include:

- American Heart Month
- International Month of Black Women in the Arts
- International Prenatal Infection Prevention Month
- LGBT History Month (United Kingdom)
- Library Lovers Month
- Marijuana Awareness Month
- National Bird-Feeding Month

"Feeding the Ducks," Mary Cassatt
For National Bird Feeding Month

- National Children's Dental Health Month
- National Haiku Writing Month
- Pet Dental Health Month
- Season for Nonviolence (January 30-April 4, worldwide)
- Spunky Old Broads Month
- Youth Leadership Month

Moveable and Multi-Day Events

Some events take place over a specific week or time period. Start and finish dates may vary from year to year. Some events occur on different days each year (such as "fourth Saturday of a month"). These events sometimes take place on February 21.

Last Tuesday (February 22-29)
- Yukon Heritage Day (Canada)

Last Friday (February 22-29)
- International Stand Up to Bullying Day

Last Saturday (February 22-29)
- Open That Bottle Night

Week Including February 22 (begins February 16-22)
- National Engineers Week (United States)

Quote of the Day

"The most serious charge which can be brought against New England is not Puritanism but February."

Joseph Wood Krutch, critic, in *The Twelve Seasons* (1949)

About
the
Month
of

February

"February," from the *Brevarium Grimani* by Simon Bening (c.1510)

February: The Second Month

The February sunshine steeps your boughs
And tints the buds and swells the leaves within.

— *William Cullen Bryant, "Among the Trees"*

The month of February takes its name from the Latin word *februum*, meaning purification, because the traditional Roman festival Februa, involving ritual purification, took place in what we now know as mid-February each year.

Because the Romans considered winter to be a monthless period, neither January nor February existed in the Roman calendar until 713 BCE, and when February did become a month, it was the last month of the year!

The number of days in February also varied in ancient times because the calendar had to be periodically adjusted to stay in line with the seasons. In some years, it was only 23 days long. When the calendar and the seasons got too far out of alignment, the Romans added a bonus month, called Intercalaris, consisting of 27 days, to bring everything back on track.

Our modern month of February begins with the calendar reforms of Julius Caesar, known as the Julian calendar. (See "On Names and Dates" for more details.) February became 28 days long, with an extra "leap day" added every four years.

Although the Julian calendar remained stable for a long time, it wasn't perfectly accurate, and the calendar gradually drifted away from the seasons again.

In 1582, under Pope Gregory XIII, the Julian calendar gave way to the Gregorian calendar, still in use today. One of the Gregorian reforms was to eliminate Leap Year when a new century was not divisible by four. As a result, 1800 and 1900 were leap years, but 2000 was not.

Although the pronunciation "feb-roo-err-ee" is preferred, the common pronunciation "feb-ew-err-ee" (as if the month was spelled "Feb-u-ary") is acceptable as well.

From the point of view of meteorologists, February is the third month of winter in the northern hemisphere and the third month of summer in the southern hemisphere.

February always starts on the same day of the week as March and November in common years, and on the same day as August in leap years. It ends on the same weekday as October in all years, and in common years also ends on the same weekday as January. In leap years, February is the only month that ends on the same day of the week as it began.

Because February is the only month with 28 days in common years, it is the only month that can pass without a single full moon. This happened in 1999 and will happen again in 2018. It is also the only month (in common years) that can have exactly four full 7-day weeks. This happens once every six years and twice every eleven years.

"February," by Joachim von Sandrart

February in Other Cultures

The month of February has different names in different
languages. Some nations use calendars other than the
Gregorian, and their months may overlap with
February. In lunar-based calendars, such as the Islamic
calendar, months move through the seasons. Still,
many languages often have a word for February itself.

Albanian: Shkurt
Anglo-Saxon: Sol-monath (cake month)
Arabic (Egypt, Sudan, Yemen): يونأغينافبراير
(fibrāyir)
Arabic (Levant): حزيركانوشباط (shubāṭ)
Arabic (Libya): الصهناالنوار (an-nuwwār)
Arabic (Algeria and Tunisia): جأيفيفري (Fīfrī)
Arabic (Morocco): غينافبراير (fibrāyər)
Azerbaijani: Fevral
Basque: Otsail
Bulgarian: февруари (fevruari)
Chinese: 二月 (Cantonese: yihyuht; Mandarin:
èryuè; Taiwanese: ji-goeh)
Corsican: Ferraghju
Croatian: Veljačaj
Czech: únor (month of submerging)
Finnish: Helmikuu (month of the pearl)
French: Février
German/Danish/Norwegian/Slovenian: Februar
Greek: Φεβρουάριος (Febrouários)
Haitian Creole: Fevriye

Hebrew: ינפבברואר (febrû'ar)
Hindi: फ़रवरी (farvarī)
Hungarian: Február
Irish (Gaelic): Feabhra mí Feabhra
Italian: Febbraio
Japanese (traditional calendar): 二月 (nigatsu); 如月 (kisaragi)
Kazakh: Ақпан (Aķpan)
Korean: 이월 (iweol)
Lithuanian: Vasaris
Maori: Hui tanguru
Old English: Solmōnaþ (mud month); Kale-monath (cabbage month)
Polish: Luty (month of ice)
Portuguese: Fevereiro
Russian: февраль (fevrali)
Scottish Gaelic: an Gearran
Sesotho: Hlakola
Spanish: Febrero
Swahili/Dutch/Swedish: Februari
Swazi: iNdlovana
Thai: Kumphaphan
Turkish: şubat
Ukrainian: лютий (ljutyj) (month of hard frost)
Vietnamese: 腡亡 (tháng ha)
Walloon: Fevrî
Welsh: Chwefror
Yiddish: פעברואַר (februar)
Zulu: uFebruwari

February Sayings and Superstitions

Here are some sayings and superstitions associated with the month of February.

February Weather Superstitions

February 12 to 14 were said to be "borrowed" from January. If those days were stormy, the year would have good weather, but if they were clear, the rest of the year would be foul.

When the cat lies in the sun in February / She will creep behind the stove in March.

Of all the months of the year / Curse a fair February.

If it thunders in February, it will frost in April.

If February give much snow / A fine summer it doth foreshow

February Wedding Superstitions

A February bride will be an affectionate wife / And a tender mother.

Married in February's sleepy weather / Life you'll tread in time together.

When February birds do mate / You wed nor dread your fate.

In Morocco, there is a ban on marriage during the seven days of *hesoum* (February 24 to March 4)

Valentine's Day Superstitions

The first man an unmarried woman sees on February 14 will be her future husband.

On Valentine's Day, if a girl writes all the names of her suitors on paper, wraps them in clay, and puts them in water, the piece that rises to the top first is the name of her husband to be.

If a woman sees a robin flying overhead on Valentine's Day, she will marry a sailor. If she sees a sparrow, she will marry a poor man but be very happy. If she sees a goldfinch, she will marry a rich person (happiness not guaranteed).

Leap Year Superstitions

Traditionally, women can propose to men on leap days, because the day had no legal status and therefor traditions did not apply. At one time, there was a Scottish law forbidding a man to refuse such a proposal. To ensure success, women should wear a red petticoat under their dress—and make sure it's partially visible to the man when they propose.

In some European countries, if a man refuses a woman's proposal on February 29, he must buy her 12 pairs of gloves.

In Scotland, it's considered unlucky to be born on a Leap Year's Day. Greeks consider it unlucky to be married during a leap year, and especially on a leap day. If you divorce during a leap year, you will never find happiness again.

February Symbols

Birthstone: Amethyst, representing piety, humility, spiritual wisdom, and sincerity

Birth Flowers: Violet and Primrose

Soviet postage stamp of an amethyst from the 1963 "Precious Stone of the Urals" series

Violet (Photo: Andrew Bossi CC BY-SA 2.5)

Still life (primroses, pears, and pomegranates),
by Henri Fantin-Latour

"February," by Eugène Grasset

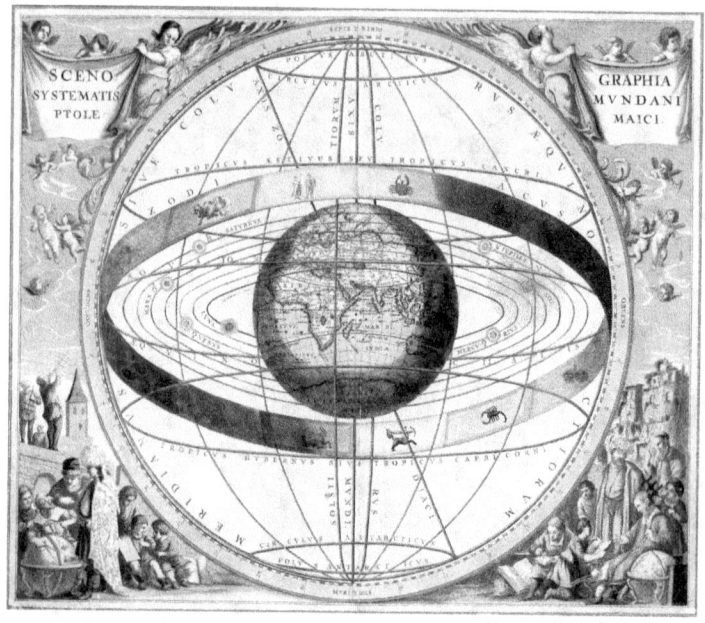

Scenography of the Ptolemaic Cosmography, by Johannes van Loon, based on Andreas Cellarius's *Harmonia Macrocosmica,* 1660

February 21 Zodiac Signs

From the perspective of someone on Earth, the Sun appears to move through the sky throughout the year, along a path astronomers call the *ecliptic plane*. The ecliptic plane is divided into twelve constellations, known as the zodiac, based on traditionally observed patterns of stars. On your birthday, you can't see your constellation, because it's in the daytime sky.

The zodiac was first developed by Babylonian astronomers about 2,500 years ago. Because they were unaware that the Earth wobbles like a spinning top (known as *precession*), they didn't make allowance for the fact that the Sun's path through the zodiac changes over time.

That means there are now two sets of dates for your birth sign. The *tropical dates* are the original Babylonian dates; the *sidereal dates* tell you where the Sun actually appears as it moves along its annual path.

For February 21, the tropical sign is **Pisces** and the sidereal sign is **Aquarius.**

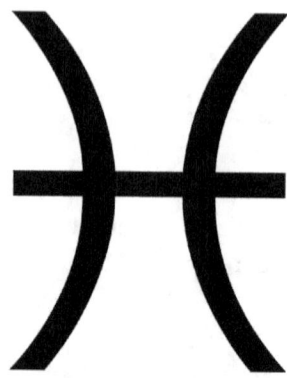

Pisces

Tropical February 20 to March 20
Sidereal March 15 to April 14

In the Roman legend of Venus and her son Cupid, they escaped the clutches of Typhon, known as the "father of all monsters," by transforming into fish and tying themselves together with rope. That's why the name Pisces is plural for fish. The constellation appears as a somewhat ragged "V" shape, representing the rope, with the "fish" located at the two rope ends.

In astrology, Pisces is a water sign, compatible with the other water signs Cancer and Scorpio, as well as with the earth signs Taurus, Virgo, and Capricorn. Pisceans are supposed to be imaginative, compassionate, unworldly, secretive, and escapist.

Aquarius

Tropical January 20 to February 19
Sidereal February 12 to March 8 (March 9 in leap years)

Aquarius is one of the oldest recognized constellations, originally representing the Babylonian god Ea. In Latin, Aquarius means "water-carrier," represented in its symbol. In Greek mythology, Aquarius is sometimes associated with Deucalion, who survived a world-cleansing flood. In Chinese astronomy, it is known as the Black Tortoise of the North (北方玄武, Běi Fāng Xuán Wǔ).

In astrology, Aquarius is considered to be masculine and extroverted, and despite the name is an air sign. Aquarians are supposed to be philanthropical, inventive, and individualistic.

Illustration by Edward Penfield

What Day of the Week is February 21?

On what day of the week does February 21 fall?

Surprisingly, this isn't an easy question. Because the calendar year is 365 days long (366 in leap years), it doesn't divide evenly by the seven days of the week.

Also, the Earth goes around the Sun in about 365-1/4 days, so a calendar tends to drift over time. That's why the same date falls on different weekdays in different years.

This is made even more complicated by a change in calendars that took place in 1582. Our modern calendar has its roots in ancient Rome, in a calendar reform conducted by Julius Caesar. Caesar commissioned mathematicians to attack the problem, and they came up with the idea of leap years, and thus standardized the calendar for centuries to come. This was called the Julian calendar.

Over time, however, the small errors in Caesar's calculation compounded. That's why Pope Gregory XIII commissioned the Gregorian calendar, used in most of the world today. Some countries converted in 1582, when the calendar was first developed; some converted later; other still haven't changed.

Gregorian and Julian aren't the only types of calendars. The Hebrew year, the Islamic year, and many other calendars are used in different parts of the world and among different people.

You can convert Gregorian dates to other calendars, including the Hebrew calendar, the Islamic calendar, and even the Mayan calendar by visiting the Fourmilab Calendar Converter at http://www.fourmilab.ch/documents/calendar/.

Chinese calendar systems are quite complex and have changed several times; a full discussion is far beyond the scope of this book. If you're interested, you can find information here: http://www.hermetic.ch/cal_stud/chinese_cal.htm.

On Names and Dates

Historians use "CE" (Common Era) and "BCE" (Before the Common Era) instead of the more common "AD" (Anno Domini, or Year of Our Lord) and "BC" (Before Christ), reflecting the fact that the year-numbering system established by the Gregorian calendar is used throughout the world in many countries not culturally Christian.

The CE/BCE designation dates back to at least 1708, and has been adopted as a standard by the United Nations and the Universal Postal Union. Because this series of books covers events and people of all nations and cultures, we use the CE/BCE terms.

The abbreviation "O.S." ("Old Style") and "N.S." ("New Style") on some dates refers to the fact that the Russian Empire (in particular) did not switch from the Julian to the Gregorian calendar at the same time as the rest of Europe, and therefore some figures and events have two dates.

Also, in the Julian calendar in England in the 16th century, the year began on March 25 rather than January 1. To avoid confusion with Gregorian dates, dates between January and March were often written using both years.

People and events whose original names are not in the Western alphabet have their native names (where possible) in the appropriate script shown in parenthesis. If you are using an e-reader to access an electronic version of this book, all characters don't always display on all devices.

A 50-year brass perpetual calendar.

Quote of the Day

"Time is an illusion, lunchtime doubly so."

Douglas Adams,
from *The Hitchhiker's Guide to the Galaxy*

Notes
and
Credits

Timespinner
Press

Cartoon by John T. McCutcheon

Copyright, Credit, and Contact

Follow Us

Our blog "This Day in History" (http://
timespinnerpress.com/this-day-in-history/) features short
articles on events and people associated with each day, and
updates several times each week. Also subscribe to the
"Quote of the Day" at http://timespinnerpress.com/quote-
of-the-day/. You can get daily links by following us on
Facebook at TimespinnerPress, or on Twitter as
@sidewisethinker.

Contact Us

Find an error or a format problem? Want information about
the series, about us, or about when the volume for your
special day might be available? Please email us at
editor@timespinnerpress.com. (We also take requests if your
special day isn't yet complete. Please give us at least six
weeks' notice if possible.)

Sources

We owe a great debt to Wikipedia, which is our first stop for
research. We attempt to make independent confirmation of
all important dates and facts through a variety of other
sources.

Other sources we frequently use include the Library of
Congress; "on this day" listings from *Encyclopedia Britannica*,
the *New York Times*, and the BBC; Omniglot for the names of
months in other languages; *Chase's Calendar of Events*; and, of
course, the always essential Google.

All art and photographs are either in the public domain, used under a Creative Commons license, or with a "fair use" justification, and most frequently come from Wikimedia Commons and the Library of Congress Prints and Photographs Division.

Attribution is provided where possible, or as requested by the copyright owner, or when there is particular historical significance, listed below. For information about any particular illustration or photograph, please contact us.

Credits

1. The cover photograph of the Washington Monument and the Reflecting Pool was taken in 2006 by Carol M. Highsmith. It is courtesy of the Carol M. Highsmith Archive collection at the Library of Congress (item 2010630248). According to the wishes of Ms. Highsmith, all photographs in that collection are in the public domain. The image has been cropped because of the dimensions of the cover.

2. The illustration of the month of February used on the back cover is from the French Gothic illuminated manuscript *Les Très Riches Heures du duc de Berry* by the Limbourg Brothers, Jean Colombe, and an intermediate painter whose name is lost to history. It is in the public domain because its copyright has expired.

3. The box graphic used on the first page is from a 1916 pamphlet entitled "Divorce versus Democracy" authored by G. K. Chesterton, originally published in London by the Society of St. Peter and St. Paul. It is in the public domain in the US because it was published prior to 1923, and is in the public domain in all countries (including the country of origin) in which the copyright time is the author's life plus 70 years or less.

4. The graphic design for the section pages in this book is from a design originally created for a pharmacy label. It is courtesy of Wellcome Images (ICV No 11073, photo V0010813), and is used here under CC BY-SA 4.0.

5. The photograph of the Washington Monument is from the National Park Service Archives, with an unknown date and photographer. It is in the public domain as a work created by an employee of the US government as part of that person's official duties.

6. The skech of the proposed Washington Monument by Robert Mills was created circa 1836 and is in the public domain because its copyright has expired.

7. The Mathew Brady/Levin Handy photograph of the partially completed Washington Monument was taken circa 1860, and is in the public domain because its copyright has expired. The image is from the Library of Congress Brady-Handy Photograph Collection, call number LC-BH823-2A.

8. The illustration of setting the aluminum apex on the Washington Monument appeared in *Harper's Weekly* magazine, December 20, 1884, page 839, and is in the public domain because its copyright has expired. It is courtesy Library of Congress (digital ID cph.3b44599).

9. The Diagram of the Principal High Buildings of the Old World is from the 1884 *Cram's Unrivaled Family Atlas of the World*, by George F. Cram. It is in the public domain because its copyright has expired.

10. The 2015 photograph "Self Recourse" is by Nebiyu Samuel, and is used here under CC BY-SA 4.0.

11. The 2004 photograph of a replica of the locomotive "Puffing Devil" by the Trevithick Society, Cornwall, United Kingdom, was taken by Chris Allen and is used here under CC BY-SA 2.0. It has been cropped.

12. The 2010 photograph of an extinct Carolina parakeet on display at the Field Museum of Natural History, Chicago, Illinois, is by James St. John, and is used here under CC BY-SA 2.0.

13. The 2010 photograph of a Polaroid 95 camera was taken by Oppidum Nissenae, and is used here under CC BY-SA 4.0.

14. The peace symbol is not an object of copyright.

15. The 1972 photograph of Mao Zedong and Richard Nixon is from the White House Photo Office, and is in the public domain as a work created by an employee of the US government as part of that person's official duties.

16. The 1964 photograph of Malcolm X was taken by staff photographer Herman Hiller for the New York *World-Telegram & Sun* (NYWTS). It is part of the NYWTS Collection at the Library of Congress (digital ID cph.3c11166). Per the instrument of gift, all photographs in that collection are in the public domain.

17. The official Congressional portrait of US Representative John Lewis is in the public domain as a work created by an employee of the US government as part of that person's official duties.

18. The official Congressional portrait of US Representative Barbara Jordan is in the public domain as a work created by an employee of the US government as part of that person's official duties.

19. The daguerreotype of Antonio López de Santa Anna was taken circa 1853 by the Meade Brothers. It is in the public domain because its copyright has expired.

20. The 1939 photograph of W. H. Auden is by Carl Van Vechten, and is part of the Van Vechten Collection at the Library of Congress (digital ID cph.3a42855). According to the Library, the image is in the public domain.

21. The 1934 publicity photograph of Ann Sheridan for *Argentinean* magazine is in the public domain because it was published in the United States between 1934 and 1977 without a copyright notice. Publicity photographs are traditionally in the public domain because of the way in which they are intended to be used.

22. The 2014 photograph of Ryan Smyth of the Edmonton Oilers is by Lisa Gansky, and is used here under CC BY-SA 2.0.

23. The portrait of Baruch Spinoza was painted by an unknown artist circa 1665, and is in the public domain because its copyright has expired.

24. The Tim Horton logo is a trademark of Tim Horton restaurants, but it is not an object of copyright. It is used here to illustrate a figure of historic significance.

25. The 1944 publicity photograph from *Creature from the Black Lagoon* is in the public domain because it was published in the United States between 1934 and 1977 without a copyright notice. Publicity photographs are traditionally in

the public domain because of the way in which they are intended to be used.

26. The 1924 photograph of Eric Liddell is in the public domain in its country of origin and elsewhere where the copyright term is the author's life plus seventy years or less.

27. The 2012 photograph of a margarita is by "Cocktail Marler," and is used here under CC BY-SA 3.0.

28. The photograph of an abandoned shopping cart is by Michiel1972, and is used here under CC BY-SA 3.0.

29. The sheet music cover for the 1914 song "Mardi Gras Rag", by Lyons and Yosco, was published by Geo. W. Meyer Music Co., New York. It is in the public domain because it was first published prior to January 1, 1923.

30. The illustration "The First Vote" by Alfred R. Waud originally appeared on the cover of *Harper's* magazine in 1867. It is in the public domain because its copyright has expired.

31. The painting "Feeding the Ducks" by Mary Cassatt was painted circa 1894 and is in the public domain because its copyright has expired.

32. The painting "February" is from the *Brevarium Grimani*, circa 1510, and is in the public domain because its copyright has expired.

33. The painting "February" by Joachim von Sandrart is in the public domain because its copyright has expired. The original can be found in the Staatsgalerie im Neuen Schloss, Schleißheim, Germany.

34. The 1815 woodcut of a proposal is in the public domain because its copyright has expired.

35. The 1896 drawing "February" by Eugène Grasset is in the public domain because its copyright has expired.

36. The 1963 Soviet postage stamp of an amethyst from the "Precious Stones of the Urals" series is not an object of copyright according to article 1259 of Book IV of the Civil Code of the Russian Federation No. 230-FZ, 12/18/2006.

37. The photograph of violets at the Abbey Church of Saint Peter, Salzburg, Austria, was taken by Andrew Bossi and used here under CC BY-SA 2.5.

38. The painting "Nature morte (primevères, poires et grenades)" by Henri Fantin-Latour is in the public domain because its copyright has expired. The original can be found at the Kröller-Müller Museum, Otterlo, Netherlands. Image courtesy Google Art Project by way of Wikimedia Commons.

39. The celestial sphere is from *Scenography of the Ptolemaic Cosmography*, by Johannes van Loon, based on Andreas Cellarius's *Harmonia Macrocosmica*, 1660. It is in the public domain because its copyright has expired.

40. The 1906 automobile calendar is by Edward Penfield, and is in the collection of the Library of Congress Prints and Photographs Division. It is in the public domain because its copyright has expired.

41. The 50-year perpetual calendar photograph is in the public domain.

42. The cartoon by John T. McCutcheon is from his 1905 collection *The Mysterious Stranger and Other Cartoons by John T. McCutcheon*. It is in the public domain because its copyright has expired.

43. The illustration "February" by Hans Thoma is from his book *Festkalender*, and is in the public domain because its copyright has expired.

Timespinner
Press

License Description and Terms

Aside from material purely in the public domain, photographs and other material in this book are used under specific licenses permitting free use, usually with an attribution requirement. For full text and terms of these licenses, click or enter the appropriate links below. If you believe there is an error in the copyright status or attribution of any of these images, please email us.

- Creative Commons Attribution 2.0 Generic (CC-BY 2.0): http://creativecommons.org/licenses/by/2.0/deed.en
- Creative Commons Attribution-Share Alike 3.0 Generic (CC-BY-SA 3.0): http://creativecommons.org/licenses/by-sa/3.0/
- Creative Commons Attribution-Share Alike 2.5 Generic (CC-BY-SA 2.5): http://creativecommons.org/licenses/by-sa/2.5/deed.en
- Creative Commons Attribution-Share Alike 2.0 Generic (CC-BY-SA 2.0): http://creativecommons.org/licenses/by/2.0/deed.en
- Creative Commons Attribution-Share Alike 1.0 Generic (CC-BY-SA 1.0): http://creativecommons.org/licenses/by-sa/1.0/deed.en
- CC0 1.0 Universal (CC0 1.0) Public Domain Dedication (CC0 1.0) http://creativecommons.org/publicdomain/zero/1.0/deed.en
- GNU Free Documentation License (GFDL): http://en.wikipedia.org/wiki/Wikipedia:Text_of_the_GNU_Free_Documentation_License
- License Art Libre (Free Art License): http://artlibre.org

"February," by Hans Thoma

Other Books from Timespinner Press

The Story of a Special Day
Michael Dobson

A series of (eventually) 366 volumes covering everything that happened on your special day! Events, births, deaths, quotes, holidays, and much more. It's like a birthday card they'll never throw away!

US$7.95 print / US$2.99 ebook.

From Plassey to Pakistan
Humayun Mirza

The history of British Colonial India and the formation of Pakistan from the unique perspective of the son of Pakistan's first president and last of the royal line of Bengal, Bihar, and Orissa! This unique historical document tells the inside story of this distinguished family, including the detailed story of the coup that toppled his father from power!

US$27.95 print

A Whole New Navy: America's War in the Pacific

Miles Durr

The most comprehensive and detailed description of America's naval war in the Pacific ever—every battle, every ship, every task force and every task group from Pearl Harbor through the Japanese surrender! A must-have for the collection of every World War II buff!

US$29.95 print

The weird, the obscure, and the strangely important

Improbable History: The Weird, the Obscure, and the Strangely Important

edited by Michael Dobson

From the birth of Western civilization to the rescue of Apollo 13, from the Leaning Tower of Pisa to Florence's Duomo, history has often turned on small, improbable details. Whatever happened to the ancient Samaritan people? Why did a fortuitous rainstorm allow the British to conquer India? How did an air raid in Italy lead to the development of chemotherapy? What happened when Albert Einstein met Adolf Hitler on the streets of Berlin? How did the Japanese manage to attack the US mainland using balloons? A cast of award-winning writers tackle some of the strangest tales in history!

US$19.95 print

www.ingramcontent.com/pod-product-compliance
Lightning Source LLC
Chambersburg PA
CBHW062052280526
45788CB00003B/1208